DON'T TRY THIS AT HOME!

The Science of Extreme Behaviors

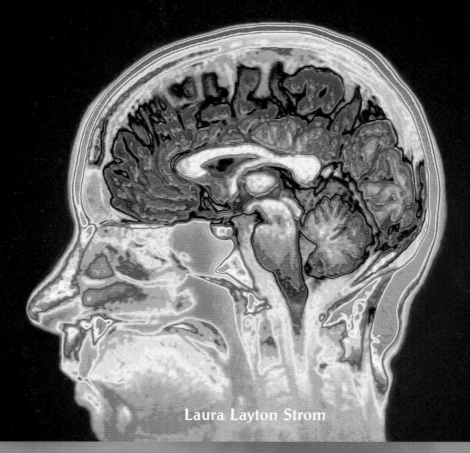

Laura Layton Strom

children's press®

An imprint of Scholastic Inc.

NEW YORK • TORONTO • LONDON • AUCKLAND • SYDNEY
MEXICO CITY • NEW DELHI • HONG KONG
DANBURY, CONNECTICUT

Library of Congress Cataloging-in-Publication Data

Strom, Laura Layton.
    Don't try this at home! : the science of extreme behaviors / by Laura Layton Strom.
      p. cm. -- (Shockwave)
    Includes index.
    ISBN-10: 0-531-17573-1 (lib. bdg.)
    ISBN-13: 978-0-531-17573-6 (lib. bdg.)
    ISBN-10: 0-531-18773-X (pbk.)
    ISBN-13: 978-0-531-18773-9 (pbk.)
1. Child welfare--Juvenile literature. 2. Children--Conduct of
life--Juvenile literature. 3. Children--Substance use--Prevention--Juvenile literature.
4. Social skills in children--Juvenile literature. I. Title. II. Series

    HV713.S84 2007
    613.8--dc22

2007012406

Published in 2008 by Children's Press, an imprint of Scholastic Inc.,
557 Broadway, New York, New York 10012
www.scholastic.com

08 09 10 11 12 13 14 15 16 17
10 9 8 7 6 5 4 3 2 1

Printed in China through Colorcraft Ltd., Hong Kong

Author: Laura Layton Strom
Educational Consultant: Ian Morrison
Editors: Jeannie Hutchins and Janine Scott
Designer: Carol Hsu
Photo Researchers: Janine Scott and Carol Hsu

Photographs by: Big Stock Photo (alcoholic drinks, pp. 30–31); **Getty Images** (p. 6–7;
pp. 10–11; drunk vagrant, pp. 20–21; p. 22; pp. 28–29); **Jennifer and Brian Lupton** (teenagers,
pp. 30–31); **Photolibrary** (pp. 12–13; firemen, pp. 16–17; pp. 18–19; MADD group, p. 21;
alcohol limit sign, p. 23); **StockXchng** (p. 3; p. 5; alcohol, pills, p. 24); **Tranz/Corbis** (cover;
p. 1; pp. 8–9; pp. 14–15; straight-line test, p. 17; handcuffed person, pp. 20–21; prohibition,
p. 23; drug education, p. 24; p. 25; pp. 26–27)

All illustrations and other photographs © Weldon Owen Education Inc.

CONTENTS

addicted physically dependent on a particular substance

alcoholism (*al kuh HOL iz uhm*) addicted to alcoholic liquor

drug a medicine or substance that has a physiological effect when taken into the body

nervous system the communication network of nerve cells that transmits nerve impulses between parts of the body

nicotine (*NIK uh teen*) a toxic, oily liquid that is found in tobacco

substance a material that can be seen or weighed. Some ——— substances, such as alcohol, can be harmful to the body.

tolerance resistance to the effect of a substance

withdrawal the reaction of the body when regular substance use is stopped

. . . .

For easy reference, see Wordmark on back flap.
For additional vocabulary, see Glossary on page 32.

The *-ism* suffix on words such as *alcoholism* means "the act of being" or "the state of." Similar words include: *criticism, optimism,* and *heroism.*

More than any other animal on the earth, humans owe their survival to the ability to learn. The human brain has an almost unlimited ability to learn, but it pays the most attention to things that are new and exciting. The brain also tends to look for cause-and-effect patterns wherever it can find them. Even though you might not be aware of how your brain works, it's constantly judging whether or not an experience is enjoyable, meaningful, and beneficial to your survival.

However, the brain can go off track. It can cause people to repeatedly do things that are bad for them. People can become **addicted** to different **substances**, such as the **nicotine** in cigarettes. They can become addicted to repetitive behaviors. This can lead people to cause harm to themselves, their family and friends, and even society as a whole. In this book, we will examine the effects of extreme behaviors on the human body.

EFFECTS OF SUBSTANCES

There are many harmful effects for people who smoke, drink, or take **drugs**.

The Individual

- A person's health can suffer in many ways. For instance, a person who smokes has a greater risk of getting heart disease and lung cancer than someone who doesn't smoke.

Friends and Family

- The person can neglect not only themselves, but also their friends and family. He or she may not carry out his or her responsibilities.

- The person may buy drugs or other substances with money intended for rent, food, or clothes.

Work and Society

- The person may make mistakes at work, leading to job loss.

- The person may steal to help pay for his or her addiction. This may lead to fines, arrests, or prison.

- The person may drive while under the influence of substances. This could lead to accidental injury or death, damage to property, fines, loss of driver's license, or prison.

7

What Is Addiction?

Addiction leads to changes in the brain. These changes in brain chemistry lead to a loss of control. They can send signals around the brain similar to those that indicate starvation. They fool the brain into thinking that it needs the addictive substance for survival.

Most addictive drugs cause the brain to feel pleasure. But over time, the brain builds a **tolerance** to the drug. That means that the drug doesn't work as well. The brain requires more and more of the drug, because it doesn't feel as good as the first time. People who are addicted may lack the self-control to quit on their own. They may continue to use the drug even if they know that it's hurting their health or their lifestyle.

SHOCKER

People who are addicted to a drug will feel **withdrawal** symptoms when the drug is taken away. If not managed properly, some forms of withdrawal can kill the addicted person!

Prescription drugs are obtained from a doctor. Used properly, they usually treat and prevent many illnesses. However, a person may become dependent on medications if they are taken over a long period of time.

Brain Drain

Some substances affect the brain and other parts of the **nervous system**. Certain substances are particularly likely to cause addiction. Drug abuse is sometimes referred to as substance abuse. Some addictive substances, however, are not illegal.

Legal Substances

- Alcohol

- Caffeine in coffee, tea, cocoa, and some soda drinks

- Inhalants, such as glue, nail polish, aerosol sprays, and gasoline

- Nicotine in cigarettes, cigars, and chewing tobacco

- Medications, such as sleeping pills or pills for pain relief (legal with a doctor's prescription)

Illegal Substances

- Synthetic, mood-altering drugs, such as amphetamines (without a doctor's prescription)

- Anabolic steroid drugs (without a doctor's prescription)

- Street drugs, such as cocaine, heroin, and marijuana

9

A Depressing Drug

Most people who use tobacco know that it's bad for them. It's estimated that 70 percent of cigarette smokers wish they could quit. Scientists have found that the more a person uses tobacco, the more likely he or she is to be depressed. Yet most people who try to quit are unable to do so. Even people who have become very sick from tobacco usually continue to use it.

Tobacco contains large amounts of nicotine, which is one of the most addictive **chemicals**. Like heroin or cocaine, nicotine causes the body to release **dopamine**, the **hormone** that causes the brain to feel pleasure. Eventually, the body produces much less dopamine without the aid of nicotine. Once addicted, a person feels the need to use tobacco almost constantly.

Did You Know?

Some people don't smoke tobacco. Instead, they put it in their mouth. Smokeless tobacco is chewed, or put between the lower lip and gum. The nicotine is absorbed by the bloodstream. Smokeless tobacco can cause mouth cancer and even lung cancer.

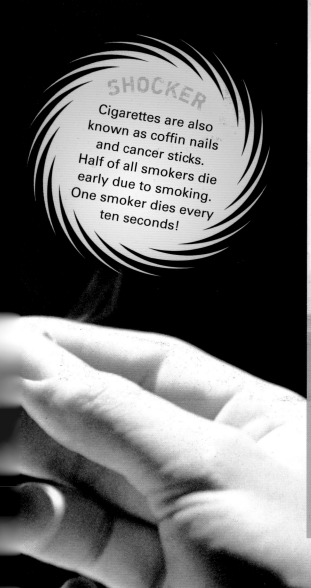

Cigarettes are also known as coffin nails and cancer sticks. Half of all smokers die early due to smoking. One smoker dies every ten seconds!

You don't have to smoke cigarettes to be affected by them. Secondhand smoke can be harmful to nonsmokers. Smoke can also affect unborn babies. **Passive smokers** can suffer from lung infections and breathing problems. Some even die from lung cancer. For every eight smokers who die, one passive smoker dies too.

Tobacco contains about 4,800 chemicals. Many of them are **toxic**. About 70 of them are known to cause cancer. Here are some chemicals found in tobacco that are also used in other products.

Acetone paint stripper

Ammonia floor cleaner

Arsenic ant poison

Carbon monoxide car-exhaust fumes

Methanol rocket fuel

Naphthalene candle wax

Nicotine addictive drug

Many countries have banned smoking in public places, such as offices, restaurants, and public transportation.

Smoking and the Body

Cigarette smoke reduces the amount of blood that reaches the brain. This may lower a smoker's IQ.

Tobacco stains teeth. The tar in tobacco causes teeth to go black. Chewing tobacco causes the gums to pull away from the teeth.

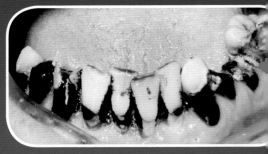

Smoker's teeth

A smoker is six times more likely to get throat cancer than is a nonsmoker.

A smoker's risk of developing heart disease is two to four times that of a nonsmoker.

Smoking damages the air sacs in the body's lungs, making it difficult to breathe. More than 80 percent of people who get lung cancer die within five years.

Nonsmoker's lung

Nicotine travels through the bloodstream and damages many other organs, causing cancers of the stomach, pancreas, kidneys, and bone marrow.

Cigarette smoke stains people's fingers and fingernails.

Smoker's lung

Tobacco use affects the body's circulation. These **thermograms** (below) show that smoking cools the body as less blood flows around it. The red area is 91 °F, the green is 86 °F, and the blue is 82 °F.

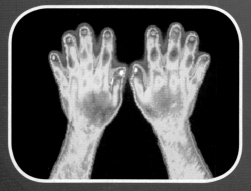

Before smoking a cigarette

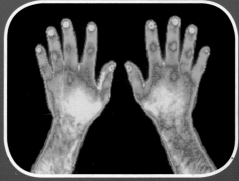

Five minutes after smoking a cigarette

Quit Smoking

There is a famous quote that says: "Giving up smoking is the easiest thing in the world. I've done it thousands of times!" Most smokers try and fail to give up smoking. In fact, about 90 percent of smokers who try to give up fail on their first attempt. Today, however, there are methods that help those who want to quit.

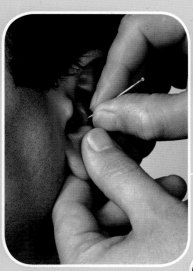

Many smokers seek medical help to stop smoking. Some find **acupuncture** or **hypnosis** can help. Acupuncturists insert needles into specific parts of the body.

Some smokers use products such as nicotine skin patches or nicotine chewing gum to help them quit smoking. Both products provide the smoker with nicotine, but without the other harmful chemicals contained in cigarettes. The nicotine in the patches and chewing gum lessen a smoker's withdrawal symptoms.

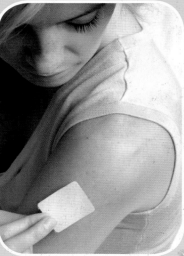

After Quitting

20 minutes
- Temperature of hands and feet increases and pulse returns to normal.

8 hours
- Carbon-monoxide levels in the blood drop to normal.

24 hours
- The chances of a heart attack decrease.

2 weeks–3 months
- Lung function improves by 30 percent and circulation improves.

1 month–9 months
- Cilia (fine hairs) in the lungs regain normal function. Coughing, tiredness, and shortness of breath decrease.

1 year
- The chances of a heart attack decrease by half.

10 years
- The chances of dying from lung cancer are now half that of a smoker.

15 years
- The chances of dying from lung cancer, heart disease, or a stroke return to nonsmoking levels.

13

Tobacco Is Big Business

If tobacco is so deadly, why is it so popular? Today, more than a billion people worldwide smoke cigarettes. That makes smoking seem normal to many people. Statistics of cancer deaths seem less real to people than the examples of people smoking without immediate visible harm.

Growing and selling tobacco is big business. It is very profitable. In the early 1600s, the American **colonies** were losing money before they started growing tobacco. More than four hundred years later, U.S. companies were selling $48.9 billion worth of tobacco. In 2002, in Kentucky alone, 30,000 farmers grew tobacco.

Many people argue that profits are less important than people's health. They point out that the costs of caring for people made sick by tobacco are $96.7 billion each year. If people stopped using tobacco, the country would save money.

The first sentence on this page is a question. I don't think the author expects an answer. I think it is her way of introducing the topic and getting the reader's attention.

SHOCKER

Low-grade tobacco leaves are used in the making of insecticides and disinfectants. Tobacco stems and stalks are used in some fertilizers.

North Carolina and Kentucky are the leading tobacco-growing areas in the United States. Each tobacco plant produces about 20 leaves and lasts for only one growing season. The leaves are picked when they ripen. Then they are **cured** in special barns. The tobacco is usually sold at auctions.

Cigarette-making machines produce about 4,000 cigarettes per minute. In the United States, about 660 billion cigarettes are produced each year. Many smokers smoke a pack (20 to 25 cigarettes) each day. So cigarette manufacturing is big business!

I miss my lung, Bob.

Anti-smoking campaigns often try to shock people. This one uses a cigarette advertising image that is familiar and somewhat glamorous, and adds a dramatic twist to call attention to the risks of smoking. In 1998, a court settlement forced the tobacco industry to pay billions of dollars toward past health-care costs and future antismoking campaigns. The manufacturers also agreed to stop marketing to young people.

Tobacco Goes Global

1000 B.C. Mayans smoke and chew tobacco.

1492 Christopher Columbus takes tobacco seeds back to Europe.

1612 John Rolfe, leader of the Jamestown colony in Virginia, brings tobacco seeds from South America. Tobacco becomes an important crop for export.

1619 European slavers begin sending African slaves to Virginia. The slaves are forced to work in tobacco fields.

1853–1856 The English are introduced to cigarettes by Turkish and Russian soldiers during the Crimean War.

1861–1865 Confederate soldiers are given rations of chewing tobacco during the Civil War.

1880 The first machine for making cigarettes is invented by American James A. Bonsack.

The Dangers of Alcohol

Alcohol is a chemical that affects the central nervous system and depresses brain functions. Alcohol is addictive. It can cause cancer, heart disease, and strokes. It can also cause malnutrition, nerve disorders, depression, **cirrhosis** of the liver, and **osteoporosis**. Alcohol use can be dangerous in the short term too. Many people are killed in alcohol-related road accidents.

It is necessary to take some risks, unless you never plan to leave the house. But alcohol reinforces the pleasure of risk-taking. It depresses the part of the brain that **inhibits** behavior, allowing people to be comfortable in situations in which they may not have been comfortable without alcohol. Alcohol also affects the part of the brain that helps you make **rational** decisions.

The following drinks contain different amounts of alcohol. The strength of an alcoholic drink is measured as a percentage.

- Beer
  (3–10 percent)

- Wine
  (8–14 percent)

- Spirits such as whiskey or vodka
  (38–45 percent)

As a person's tolerance increases, he or she has to consume more and more alcohol before feeling "drunk."

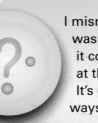

I misread the word *inhibit*. I thought it was *inhabit*. I went back and reread it correctly. Then I used the glossary at the back of the book just to check. It's great how you can use different ways to figure out new words.

In the United States, it is illegal to drive with a blood-alcohol content (BAC) of 0.08 or more, which is a limit of 80 mg of alcohol per 100 ml of blood. Police officers often ask drivers suspected of drinking to walk along a straight line. It is a quick way to tell if the person is under the influence of alcohol. Officers also use breathalyzers, which measure a person's BAC. Often the police set up checkpoints where they can randomly test drivers.

Many people who have been drinking believe that they are capable of driving safely. However, alcohol plays a major role in one-fourth of all fatal traffic accidents. **Binge** drinking or drinking to get drunk kills about 300 Americans each year.

Alcohol and Behavior

The greater the intake of alcohol, the greater the effect on the body.

1. Lowered inhibitions
2. Some loss of muscular coordination
3. Decreased alertness
4. Impaired ability to drive
5. Increased loss of coordination
6. Slowed reaction time
7. Clumsiness and exaggerated emotions
8. Unsteadiness
9. Hostile or aggressive behavior
10. Slurred speech
11. Inability to walk
12. Confusion
13. Incapacitation, loss of feeling
14. Inability to wake up
15. Unconsciousness
16. Coma
17. Death from organ (lung, heart) failure if not treated

Alcohol and the Brain

Cerebral cortex

Alcohol depresses the cerebral cortex, the part of the brain that controls thinking and processing information from the senses. When drunk, a person will lose the ability to think clearly and make good decisions. He or she will have trouble seeing, hearing, smelling, touching, tasting, and feeling pain.

Hypothalamus

Alcoholism can deplete vitamin B in the brain. This can lead to depression, **apathy**, **amnesia**, and loss of motor control, and can cause the person to have false memories.

Limbic system

As alcohol affects the limbic system, the person is subject to exaggerated states of emotion, such as anger and aggressiveness. He or she may also suffer from short-term and long-term memory loss.

Cerebellum

Alcohol affects the cerebellum, the part of the brain that controls balance and coordination.

Pituitary gland

Long-term drinking can cause people to feel lonely and mistrustful. Alcohol decreases levels of oxytocin, a chemical released by the brain. Oxytocin is believed to help people form emotional bonds.

Medulla

The medulla controls essential bodily functions, such as breathing and heart rate, and regulates body temperature. Too much alcohol will cause a person to feel sleepy, lose consciousness, or even stop breathing.

Brain Activity

When a person stops drinking alcohol, his or her brain activity increases. This scan of an alcoholic's brain (right) shows how the brain gets more active the longer the person goes without alcohol. High activity in the brain is shown in yellow.

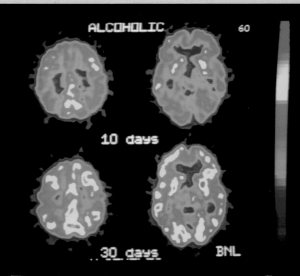

ALCOHOLIC   60

10 days

30 days   BNL

Alcohol and the Body

Alcohol can raise the level of some fats in the blood and can lead to high blood pressure as well. It can also weaken the walls of the heart, leading to heart attacks.

Alcohol can also cause ulcers and stomach cancer.

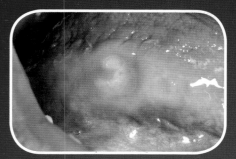

Tongue ulcer

The liver's job is to filter toxins out of the bloodstream. It's up to the liver to remove alcohol. Drinking overtaxes the liver, causing it to become fat and less efficient. Long-term drinking causes cirrhosis (scarring of the liver) and hepatitis, which are often fatal.

Cirrhosis of the liver

The pancreas regulates the amount of sugar in the blood. Alcohol can damage the pancreas, leading to diabetes.

A person who has had too much alcohol one day may experience a hangover the next. Alcohol dehydrates the body, causing a headache. The person may also feel sick and have a dry mouth.

Problems That Alcohol Brings

Alcohol causes health problems, and it's also blamed for bad behavior and poor decision making. People who drink alcohol are more likely to harm themselves or others, and are more likely to be arrested. About 30 to 90 percent of all violent crimes are committed while under the influence of alcohol. People are more likely to attack strangers, friends, and family members while drinking.

Drinking during pregnancy can cause a birth defect in babies called fetal alcohol syndrome (FAS). For hundreds of years, people have been warned not to drink while pregnant. Today, FAS is the leading cause of mental retardation.

People with severe drinking problems may lose track of where they are. They may tumble to the ground and fall asleep in a dangerous spot.

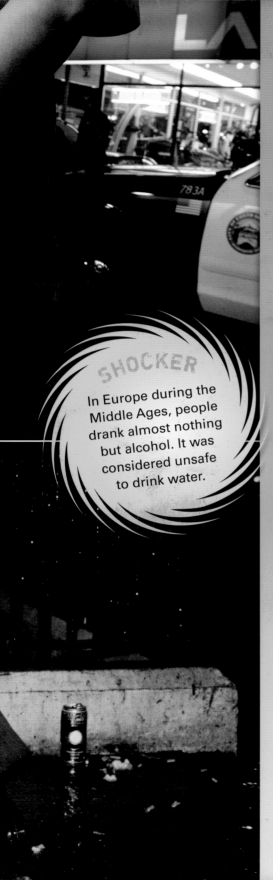

In Europe during the Middle Ages, people drank almost nothing but alcohol. It was considered unsafe to drink water.

Against Drunk Driving

Mothers Against Drunk Driving (MADD) is a nonprofit organization. It was founded by Candy Lightner of California. Her thirteen-year-old daughter was killed by a drunk driver on May 3, 1980. MADD's aim is to stop drunk driving, to offer support to victims, and to save lives. Here people attend an annual candlelight memorial to remember loved ones lost or injured in alcohol-related crashes.

Dangerous Drinking

Because the abuse of alcohol causes harm to entire societies, most governments have policies to protect people from alcohol-related crimes and traffic accidents. In the United States, it's a serious crime to drive a car while under the influence of alcohol. It's also illegal to sell alcohol to anyone under the age of twenty-one. The government also places high taxes on alcohol to make it less affordable. The hope is that if alcohol is too expensive, people will drink less.

Some people want the government to do even more. They point out that companies that sell alcohol encourage people to drink excessively. Some people think that irresponsible advertising should be illegal. Some areas in the United States have banned alcohol altogether. But studies show that people drink just as much in those areas as they do elsewhere.

Did You Know?

At the time of the Italian explorer Marco Polo (1254–1324), taxes on alcohol represented one of the Chinese emperor's biggest sources of income.

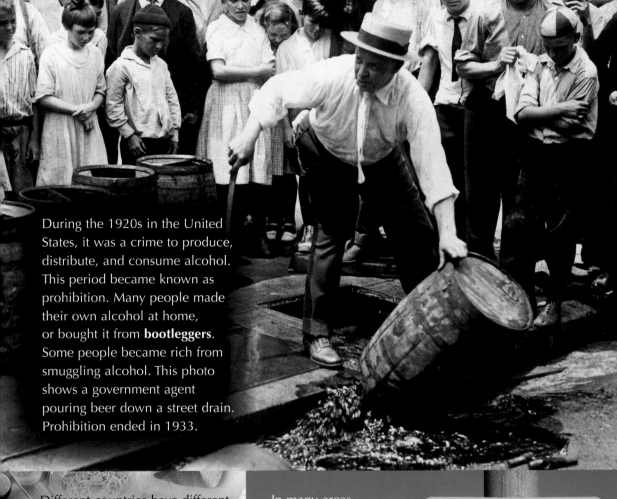

During the 1920s in the United States, it was a crime to produce, distribute, and consume alcohol. This period became known as prohibition. Many people made their own alcohol at home, or bought it from **bootleggers**. Some people became rich from smuggling alcohol. This photo shows a government agent pouring beer down a street drain. Prohibition ended in 1933.

Different countries have different attitudes toward alcohol. In places such as Italy and France, people are exposed to alcohol from a young age. Small amounts of alcohol are considered healthy. Wine is usually served at every meal, even to teenagers. But binge drinking is strongly discouraged. Italian teenagers are only one-tenth as likely to abuse alcohol as U.S. teenagers.

In many areas, there are signs to remind people about the legal drinking limits and the consequences of ignoring them.

ALCOHOL .08% LIMIT

Suspended = NO Exceptions

Limiting Alcohol Use

- no driving while under the influence
- no selling alcohol to people under 21
- high taxes on alcohol
- total alcohol ban in some places

PAY

Deeper Into the Habit

As a person becomes more addicted to substances such as nicotine or alcohol, the brain produces less dopamine naturally. Feelings of depression increase. This can drive people to even more drastic substance use. They might smoke or drink more and more. Or they might start using more serious drugs, such as illegal street drugs. They might abuse prescription medication, or misuse household products to get high.

Drug use that seems fun and sociable at first can cause a person to become seriously isolated later. As more and more of an addict's life is dedicated to his or her drug, he or she may start to feel that nonusers "just don't get it." Addicts may feel hostile to nonusers. They may be ashamed of their habits, and withdraw from society in order to hide their behavior. A person who once drank at parties may now decide to hide out at home with a drink.

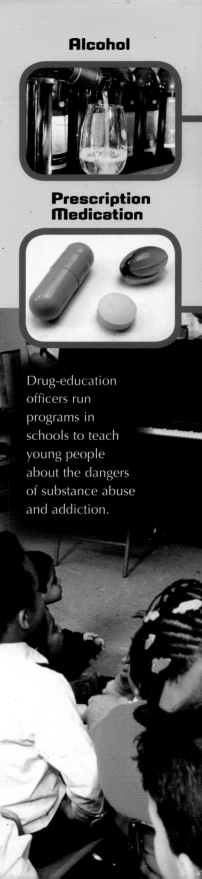

Alcohol

Prescription Medication

Drug-education officers run programs in schools to teach young people about the dangers of substance abuse and addiction.

The Five Stages of Addiction

1. Use	2. Misuse	3. Abuse	4. Dependence	5. Addiction
drinking one glass of wine at dinner	getting drunk at parties	hiding a drinking habit from friends and family	drinking alone every night	physical need to start drinking at the same time every day
taking pain medication as given by a doctor	taking more pills each time than the doctor prescribed	faking pain to get a new prescription	failing to fall asleep without the medication	consuming need to keep taking the pills; refusal to stop

? I'm glad the author included a chart. As I was reading the left-hand page, I kept glancing toward the chart. It helped me understand what I was reading.

People can become dependent on things other than drugs. Some people feel the need to drink excessive amounts of a particular brand of soda every day. Other people work long hours. Some people neglect their friends, family, and education in order to watch television all day long. People have ruined their finances while trying to satisfy a gambling habit.

A Healthy Attitude

Playing sports and dancing release **endorphins** in the brain. These chemicals help you feel good in a natural way.

Scientists know that people who are depressed are more likely to engage in extreme behavior. But it works the other way around too. Substance addictions can also cause depression. It's been proven that cigarette smokers are often depressed by the damage they're doing to their bodies.

Psychologists know that a healthy attitude toward life makes a person less vulnerable to substance addiction. They encourage people to be passionate about life, and to pursue a wide range of interests. Even a good thing, such as schoolwork, can be unhealthy if it causes you stress or low self-esteem.

It's also important to have confidence. Sometimes it's necessary to say unpopular things, or speak up when someone makes you angry. People who suppress emotions are more likely to turn to alcohol and other substances that let them feel artificially brave.

Brain Food

Here are some things that you can do to enjoy life and keep your brain active and healthy.

You can learn to cook. Good food causes complex reactions in the brain. Over time, your sense of taste will improve.

You can learn a foreign language. Speaking different languages teaches the brain to be more flexible.

Cause	Effect
• depression	• extreme behavior
• extreme behavior	• depression
• healthy attitude	• less likely to develop substance addiction
• exercise	• feeling good

Bouncing Back

Everyone is dependent on different things. The brain latches onto behavior that seems to work. But when dependence turns into addiction, it's time for a cure. Bigger addictions require bigger solutions. It's important to get advice from trustworthy adults.

Addicts can overcome their patterns of unhealthy behavior. The brain has a tremendous ability to recover. It can learn new patterns. It can regrow damaged brain cells. But the longer a person has been addicted to a substance, the harder it is to stop. He or she must take steps to recover. An addict can follow treatments prescribed by experts.

Some governments require that people receive treatment for their addictions. As long as the treatments are followed, addicts can recover.

Getting Help

If someone you know has a problem with addiction, the following groups can help.

Narcotics Anonymous (NA) is a global support organization for people who have a problem with drugs.

Alcoholics Anonymous (AA) is a global support organization that offers help to people who want to stop drinking.

Al-Anon and Alateen are global support organizations for family and friends affected by someone's drinking.

The word *anonymous* comes from the Greek word *anonymos*, meaning "without a name." Members of Alcoholics Anonymous do not have to reveal their full names.

If you believe that a friend has a problem with substance abuse, here are a few practical steps you could take:

· Learn about the symptoms of substance abuse. If your friend displays any of these, he or she might have a problem.

· Before talking to your friend, make a list of reasons why your friend may need help. Take care not to blame or judge your friend.

· If your friend gets angry or denies that he or she has a problem, end the conversation. Instead, talk to a trusted adult about the situation. It may be wise to work with an adult to organize a meeting called an intervention. At an intervention, friends and family gather to convince the person to seek help. Before you stage an intervention, meet with a professional counselor to plan exactly what you will say to your friend.

29

In the United States, the government has varying views regarding the age of adulthood. At the age of eighteen, young people are trusted to vote and to fight in wars. However, although an eighteen-year-old can use guns in war, he or she is considered too young to own them.

In most of the U.S., the legal age to enter into a contract is eighteen. In most states, people can marry at age eighteen without parental consent.

WHAT DO YOU THINK?

Do you think that eighteen-year-olds should be trusted to make all decisions about their health and welfare?

PRO

I think the legal age for anything should be eighteen. If someone is old enough to fight in a war, they should be trusted to make other important decisions.

The legal age to buy cigarettes in most states is eighteen. To drink alcohol legally in the United States, a person must be twenty-one. Yet in some countries, such as China, there is no drinking age. In France, the drinking age is sixteen. In Mexico, it is eighteen.

CON

I think that the legal age for most things should be eighteen. But I think the legal age for alcohol should stay at twenty-one. Alcohol affects people's judgment. No one under twenty-one outside the military should be allowed to own a gun.

Go to **www.kidshealth.org/ kid/stay_healthy/body/ alcohol.html** to learn more about alcohol and the body.

acupuncture (*AK yoo pungk chur*) a way of treating illness by pricking specific parts of the body with small needles

amnesia (*am NEE zhuh*) partial or total loss of memory

apathy (*ap uh THEE*) lack of interest in or enthusiasm about something

binge (*BINJ*) characterized by excess or compulsion

bootlegger a person who illegally makes and sells alcohol

chemical (*KEM uh kuhl*) related to, or produced by, chemistry, which is the study of substances

cirrhosis (*suh ROH sihss*) a chronic disease of the liver

colony (*KOL uh nee*) a settlement under the rule of a parent country

cure to dry the sap from harvested tobacco leaves

dopamine (*DOH puh meen*) a chemical that acts in the brain to influence feelings and behaviors

endorphin (*en DOR fin*) a chemical produced by the body, which reduces pain and can improve mood

hormone a chemical made in the body that affects the way a person grows, develops, or behaves

hypnosis (*HIP noh siss*) the induction in a person of a trancelike state in which the subject becomes vulnerable to suggestion or direction from someone else

inhibit to prevent or hinder

osteoporosis (*oss tee oh puh ROH sihss*) a condition in which bones become fragile

passive smoker a nonsmoker who involuntarily inhales smoke from another person's cigarette, cigar, or pipe

psychologist (*sye KOL uh jist*) someone who studies the human mind, its functions, and the way people behave

rational (*RASH uh nuhl*) logical or sensible

thermogram (*THUR moh gram*) a record made by an instrument that records the varying temperatures of an area

toxic (*TOK sik*) poisonous